Butterflies fluttering in the sky, spott[e] by, grasshoppers, bumblebees, roly- and more are featured in brightly col[o]. and whimsical verse. The simple text, vibrant palette, actual size bug chart, and bug-o-meter will have all backyard entomologists buzzing with excitement.

Praise for *Bugs! Bugs! Bugs!*

"Will be a hit at storytime." —*School Library Journal*

"A bug lover's delight." —*Booklist*

"The butterfly-bright multimedia artwork . . . makes this book soar." —*Publishers Weekly*

A Texas 2x2 Reading List selection
A Parents' Choice Recommended Seal

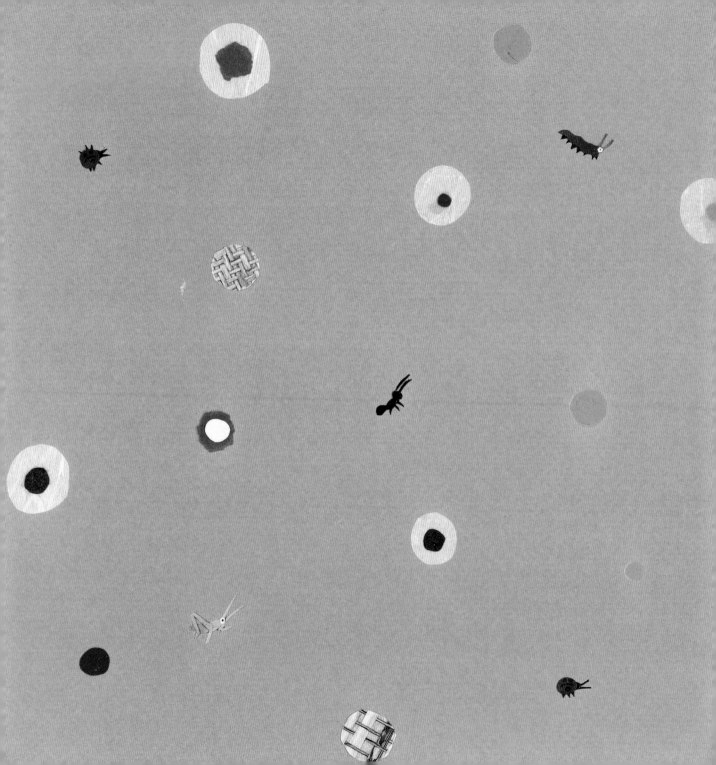

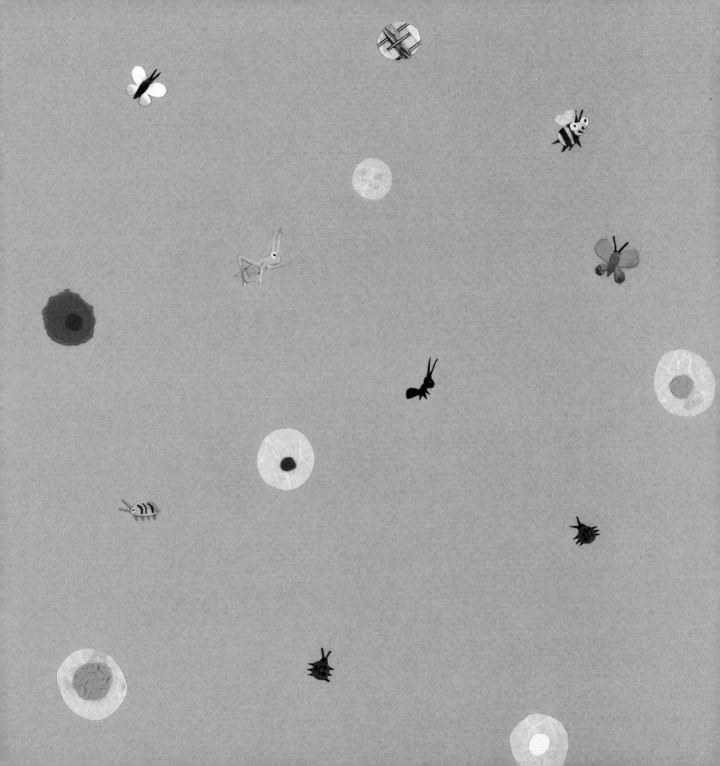

For my aunts. — B.B.

First Chronicle Books LLC paperback edition, published in 2017.
Originally published in hardcover in 1999 by Chronicle Books LLC.

ISBN 978-1-4521-6137-2

The Library of Congress has cataloged the original edition as follows:
Barner, Bob.
Bugs! Bugs! Bugs! / by Bob Barner.
p. cm.
Summary: A nonsense rhyme introduces children to familiar bugs. Includes a fun facts section.
ISBN 978-0-8118-2238-1
1. Insects—Juvenile literature. [1. Insects.] I. Title.
QL467.2.B365 1999
595.7—DC21
98-39604   CIP
           AC

Manufactured in China.

MIX
Paper from
responsible sources
FSC™ C104723
www.fsc.org

Book design by Jennifer West.
Typeset in Tweed.
The illustrations in this book were rendered in paper collage.

10 9 8 7 6 5 4 3 2 1

Chronicle Books LLC
680 Second Street
San Francisco, California 94107

Chronicle Books—we see things differently.
Become part of our community at www.chroniclekids.com.

Bugs! Bugs! Bugs!

by

Bob Barner

chronicle books · san francisco

Bugs! Bugs! Bugs!

I want to see bugs!

Butterflies that

flutter in the sky

Spotted ladybugs

that go creeping by

Friendly
daddy longlegs

that never bite

Grasshoppers hop

hop, hopping
out of sight

A fuzzy caterpillar

with tiny feet

Bees buzzing by flowers that smell so sweet...

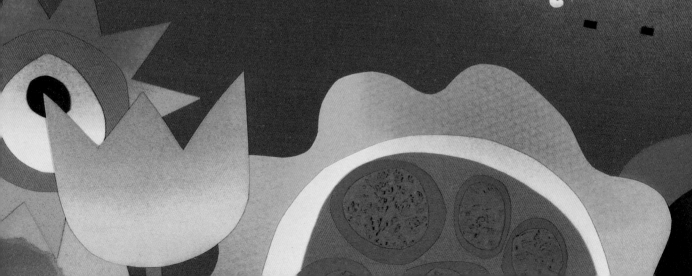

A long line of ants

that work so much

Roly-poly bugs

I can see buggy bugs all around me!

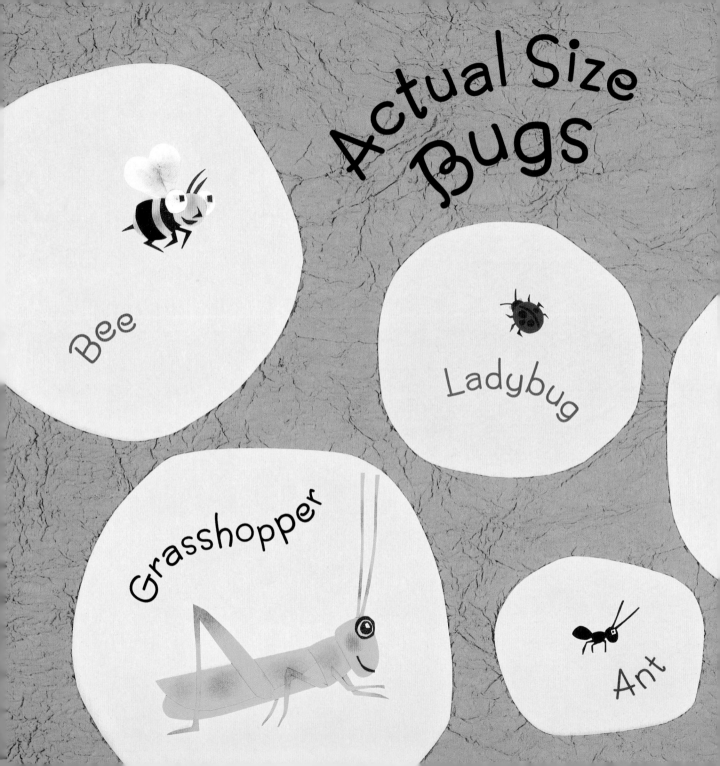

Actual Size Bugs

Bee

Ladybug

Grasshopper

Ant

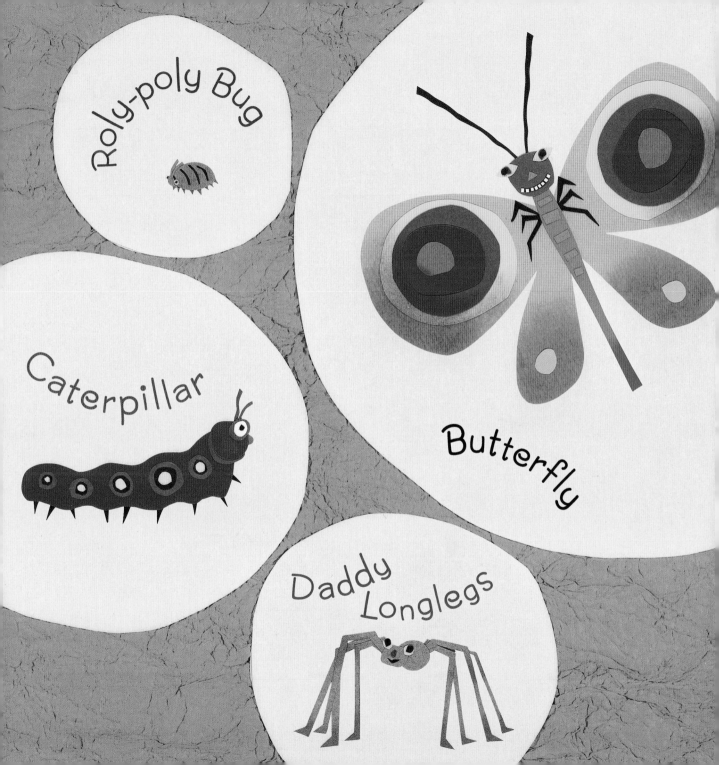

Roly-poly Bug

Butterfly

Caterpillar

Daddy Longlegs

Bug-O-Meter

	Butterfly	Ladybug	Daddy Longlegs
Can it fly?	Yes	Yes	No
Where does it live?	Near flowers	On plants	In shady spots
How many legs?	6	6	8
Does it sting?	No	No	No

Grasshopper	Caterpillar	Bee	Ant	Roly-poly Bug
Yes	No	Yes	No	No
In tall grass	On twigs & leaves	Near flowers	Ant hill	Under rocks
6	6-16	6	6	14+
No	No	Yes!	Yes, sometimes	No

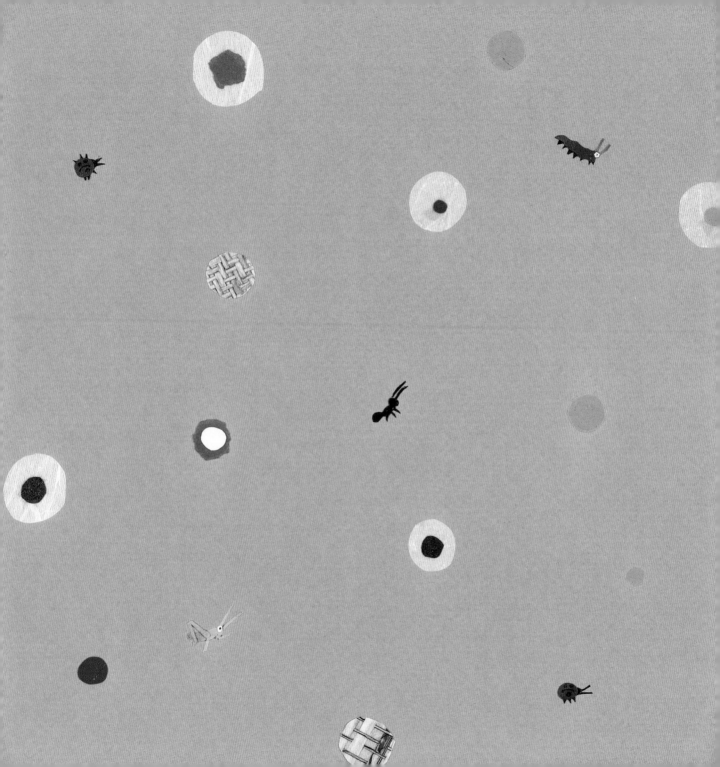

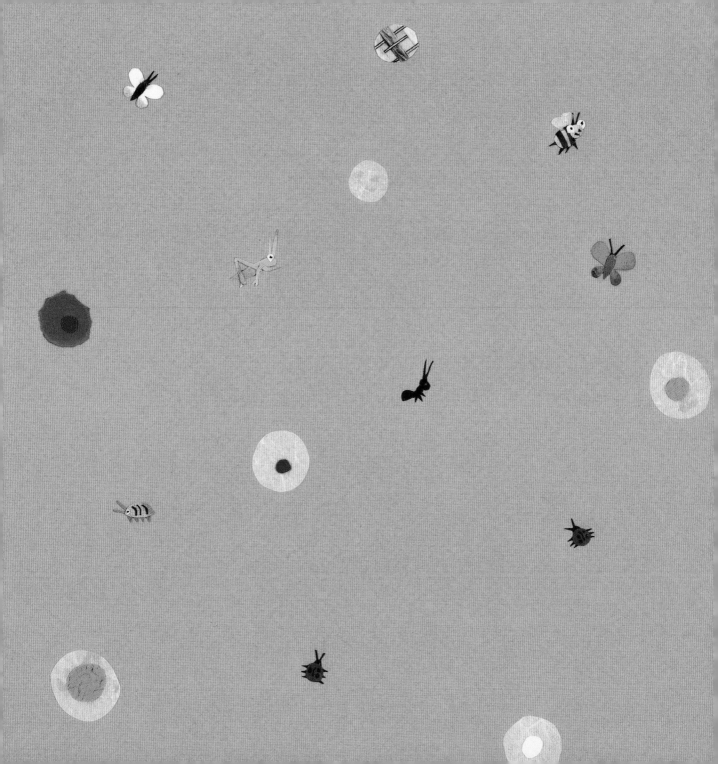

Bob Barner was born in Arkansas, grew up in the Midwest, and now lives in San Francisco. He received a bachelor of fine arts degree from the Columbus College of Art & Design in Columbus, Ohio. In addition to creating art, Bob enjoys teaching and visits many schools and libraries to talk about his work. Bob's favorite bug is a roly-poly but his least favorite bug is a silverfish. To learn more about Bob, please visit www.bobbarner.com.

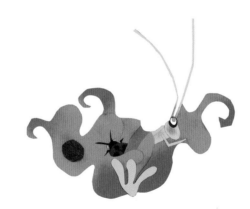